# What Wants to Come Through Me Now

# What Wants to Come Through Me Now

## Rabindranath Tagore's
*Gitanjali* (Song Offerings)

### A New Translation/Version
by Coleman Barks

FONS VITAE

First published in 2020 by
Fons Vitae
49 Mockingbird Valley Drive
Louisville, KY 40207
http://www.fonsvitae.com
Email: fonsvitaeky@aol.com

Library of Congress Control Number: 2020946662
ISBN 978-1891785-047

Printed in Canada

# Contents

# Introduction : Constant Communion

Rabindranath Tagore is one of the great universal mystics. As you read his *Gitanjali* (Song Offerings), you feel the depth and the honesty of his experience, "the great lifelong adventure," he calls it. "We are in the process of being created. We may not know exactly what is happening. But we feel the flow of life in us to be one with the universal life outside. The relation of my soul to this beautiful autumn morning, this vast radiance, is one of intimate kinship; and all this colour, scent, and music is but the outward expression of our secret communion. This constant communion, whether realized or unrealized, keeps my mind in movement; out of this intercourse between my inner and outer world I gain such religion, be it much or little, as my capacity allows: and in its light I have to test the scriptures before I can make them really my own" (Glimpses, 87). These comments from a letter he wrote on Oct. 5, 1895, come from a time when he was still "under the shelter of obscurity," enjoying "the greatest freedom my life has ever known." He thrived best in the anonymous privacy of not being famous. These poems were written from within that shelter. We feel in them the extravagant intimacy of his communion with his soul. That may be our primary response to this sequence of poems. I know it is my own. I recognize in his poetry my own feeling of inner freedom and soul friendship, along with the flooding joy of expressing that, all within a relaxed playfulness. If I may be so grandiose. I certainly do not claim his breadth of interior life. I just feel I can read many of his poems with empathy, and with some understanding.

Ironically, in that regard, it was this little book that propelled him out onto the wide field of the world's attention. It brought him the Nobel Prize. Published in Bengali in 1910, Tagore's *Gitanjali* was published in English in England by a small publishing house in 1912 and then by Macmillan in March of 1913. This *Gitanjali* (Song

Offerings) was Tagore's own prose translation from his mother tongue Bengali. It was all the Swedish Academy had to judge him by when, later that year, they awarded him the Nobel Prize for Literature, on Nov. 13, 1913. He was the first Asian to receive that honor. It certainly helped that W.B. Yeats had written an enthusiastic introduction to Tagore's collection. This edition is still available from Macmillan, and elsewhere. It is the text I have worked from to make these versions. Why do such a thing, you ask? Why make a "version," you might ask? Sometimes his insights, which feel very natural and true, seem lost behind some clunky Edwardian language-furniture. By which I mean, for example: "frail vessel," "respite," "my work becomes an endless toil on a shoreless sea of toil," "the bees plying their minstrelsy." And sometimes, though what is being said is not fake-holy, the wording of it might sound like that to us. The "Thees" and "Thous," "the fleeting moment," "starry gems," "uttermost beauty," and "abidest."There are also examples of dead wording from minor Victorian poetry: "dim," "weary," "gaze," "ablaze," "a-tremble," "things I have ever spurned," "in toil and in the sweat of my brow." So I am trying here to rephrase his insights in language that does not cloud their brilliance. Tagore's mysticism feels very simple and abundant (Yeats' adjectives for it), like Wordsworth's, like Whitman's, like Galway Kinnell, Robert Hass, like the clear, passionate visions of Franz Wright and his father James. It is into that more current idiom, that *American* beauty, that I am trying to place Tagore's songs.

In a letter to Ezra Pound on January 5, 1913, Tagore admitted that "I do not know the exact value of your English words. Some of them may have their souls worn thin by constant use and some others may not have acquired their souls yet. So in my use of words there must be some lack of proportion and appropriateness perhaps, that also could be amended by friendly hands" (Anthology, 156). It sounds like he is asking Ezra for help. Good choice (Pound). But Pound did not help Tagore revise the English of the *Gitanjali* as he (Pound) did so magnificently with Eliot's *The Waste Land*.

There was a rumor, however, after Tagore received the Nobel Prize, and persisting to this day, that Yeats had rewritten Tagore's English prose translation of the *Gitanjali*. Yeats himself in private correspondence had given some credence to the notion. "William Rothenstein (to whom the *Gitanjali* is dedicated) will tell you how much I did for *Gitanjali*. It was a delight. And at my request Tagore has made no acknowledgment." But Rothenstein specifically discounted the rumour in his memoirs. "Yeats did here and there suggest slight changes, but the main text was printed as it came from Tagore's hands" (Myriad, 184, top). Wendy Barker, in talking about Yeats' typescript of the *Gitanjali* in the Berg Collection in the New York Public Library, mentions only some very minor mistakes that Yeats made in regard to Bengali compound nouns (Final Poems, xxi), no substantive changes, so the idea that the *Gitanjali* is in any way Yeats' text can be discounted.

Being a century away from the event now, we may not be able to gauge the profound and exotic impression made on the English literary world in 1912 by the appearance of Tagore and his *Gitanjali*.

We have many descriptions of it. The poet Thomas Sturge Moore was at the famous soirée of July 7, 1912. He privately told Yeats then that he found Tagore's poetry "preposterously optimistic." Yeats replied, "Ah, you see, he is absorbed in God." Sturge Moore later became a loyal friend of Tagore's. He was, in fact, the one responsible for recommending Tagore to the Swedish Academy for the Nobel Prize.

Twenty years later in his last letter to Yeats, Tagore remembered those early days in England: "I felt that I had come to the beginning of a fresh existence, young with the surprise of an experience in an atmosphere of kindly personalities."* Ernest Rhys, editor of the Everyman Library, who wrote the first biography of Tagore in English (1915), mentions "a famous English critic" of the day who said, "I have met several people, not easily impressed, who could not read that book (RT's *Gitangjali*) without tears. As for me, I read a few pages and then put it down, feeling it too good for me. The rest of it I mean to read in the next world . . .." This ecstatic charisma was also felt in the man's presence as well. On October 12, 1912, Tagore had lunch with Ezra Pound, then spent the afternoon with him discussing prosody and reciting and singing his own poetry. Pound said that Tagore made him feel "like a painted Pict with a stone war-club." The exotic effect of Tagore's physical presence can hardly be overestimated. The poet Robert Bridges said, "Tagore is an extraordinarily good-looking fellow. There is

---

* The source for this and many other of these references may be found in the magnificently researched biography, *Rabindranath Tagore: The Myriad-Minded Man*, Krisha Dutta and Andrew Robinson, Tauris Parke Paperbacks, 2009; first published by Bloomsbury Publishing, 1995.

something unreal about him, something Assyrian, Old Asiatic. Do you think he puts gold in his beard?" The sense of a numinous aura was strong. Tagore is often compared to Jesus.

Yet there are other responses too. His good friend William Rothenstein tells Ernest Rhys around this time (1914), "Tagore has not really found peace. And it is because he hasn't, because he feels the same impossibility of reconciling action with thought that there is so much reality and passion in his songs. Perhaps he feels more strongly than most men the need for peace, but he has found no road where he can walk safely." It is this restlessness that gives his poems such a trembling vitality, and such a human fibre to his mysticism. This is a very penetrating literary insight of Rhys'.

In the *Fortnightly Review* Pound said about the *Gitanjali*, "Briefly, I find in these poems a sort of ultimate common sense, a reminder of one thing and of the forty things of which we are likely to lose sight in the confusion of our Western life, in the racket of our cities, in the jabber of manufactured literature, in the vortex of advertisement." Pound goes on for nine pages. His only critical remark is that the general reader might find the poems "too pious." Then Pound rejects this. "I have nothing but pity for the reader who is unable to see that their piety is the poetic piety of Dante, and that it is very beautiful." That from one of the most stringent critical minds in the West. The *Times Literary Supplement* reviewed the *Gitanjali*, "He is so simple that anyone can understand him; yet this does not mean that there is little to understand."

The list of writers that spoke enthusiastically, and publicly, about Tagore's work is impressive. Yeats, Robert Bridges, Gide, Saint-John Perse, Jimenez, Anna Akhmatova, Ezra Pound, Wilfred Owen, Edward Thomas, Hart Crane, and Robert Frost. Yeats perhaps sums up what the Western literary community felt with his own personal response. "A whole people, a whole civilization, immeasurably strange to us, seems to have been taken up into this imagination, and yet we are not moved because of its strangeness, but because we have met our own image, . . . or heard, perhaps for the first time in literature, our voice as in a dream" (Yeats' Introduction, 11).

What was this so-familiar dream-voice saying? For one thing (#14) that the great abundant gifts that come to him (Tagore) unasked-for, those which save him from his own confused and excessive desiring, and from what is most destructive (a weak, uncertain love)are these: the sky, the light, his body, and his mind. These absolutely basic, magnificent, realities give him focus and a shape, and let him be worthy and open to what such gifts bring. The simple abundance he feels gets clearer when he writes of childhood and infancy. See #60, #61, and #62. Also #97. These particular poems seem more free and playful than the rest. The best statement on playfulness may be #43. In that poem, by the way, I change Tagore's "playroom" to "backyard," because that was my own childhood kingdom. #95, the threshold poem, the boundaries of birth and death, is also important to this theme, with the final, wonderful, nursing image. My teacher, Bawa Muhaiyaddeen, when asked what it felt like to be him, answered by imitating a baby's suckling at the mother's breast. *Yum-yum-yum.* There is a lovely joy and deep playfulness in Tagore's poems. There is also a sadness that he seems to be in love with. He will not give it up. In his surrender to the mystery, he says that the giving up of his sadness will come at the very last.

Some of the most attractive sections, to me, of this poem sequence are those that tell small stories. They have the feel of bits of homemade myth. For example:

#64 – A man lives in a dark house. A woman comes by with a lamp. During the course of a night he asks her, three times, to bring her light into his house. She refuses each time, for different reasons. Here is her last refusal.

> *This lamp is meant to join*
> *with the great carnival of lights.*

> I watch her light get uselessly lost
> among a hundred others.

#54 – A man by a well is lost in "vague musings." Some women invite him to join them. He drifts off. No answer. A mystical presence comes. *I am a thirsty traveler.* The man rouses and pours some water into the man's hands cupped together for a bowl. The presence asks his name. The man is filled with wonder and shame. *Why would you* want to know my name? Yet the memory of that asking is a sweetness that enfolds him. Then he goes back to his "thoughts."

#48 – A busy, beautiful, morning, with friends in a hurry to set out. Where? No one knows. About noon the speaker gets tired and lies down in the grass. His friends laugh at his tiredness and leave him behind. He says their mockery almost got him up, but not. He lies back "in glad humiliation, sun-threaded green air spreading through my psyche." He calls it a surrendering again "to shadow and song and sleep." He wakes from this sublime relaxation into the presence that so many of these poems seem to be waiting for.

Now I wake to see you flooding into me your smile.

I had so wrongly thought the way was long
>        and difficult, the one
>        that reaches into your presence.

#50 – A beggar is visited in the midst of his door to door begging by a glorious sun-presence. He thinks his luck is about to change. But the presence asks him, "What will you give *me*?" Confused, he feels in his bag, finds a tiny corn grain, and gives the sun-presence that. Later, at the end of his day, he empties out his bag. In the pitiful trash heap there is small nugget of pure gold just the size of the corn grain. He weeps for his lack of generosity. "I should have given you my soul, my life."

Most of these stories are more mysterious, and less conclusive, than this one. Pound, in fact, pointed to this one as "too didactic" for his taste.

#52 – A woman is speaking. It is morning and her love, her lord, has left the bed and gone. "What has he left me?" she muses. "A flower, a vase of perfumed water?" "No. You have left me your sword, like a living flame." A bird lights in the window and asks, "What has he given you?" "This gift that is too heavy to carry. You have given me death as a friend to walk with. This keen discernment. No more waiting, no fear. Nothing can bind me now."

*The lord of my heart wants no decoration,*
>        *nothing flirtatious, nothing coy.*

*No doll clothes nonsense.*
>        *I have my sword.*

#57 – A small village is closing up for the night. Someone says, "The king is coming." Impossible, they think. Such a thing cannot be. During the night they hear various sounds, but they disregard them all. At dawn, they discover that the king and his retinue are actually at their gate. There is no time to prepare. They must welcome him with what they have, which is nothing.

There is a voice in these poems that is very at ease in its conversation with mystery. #1 – *It pleases you that you have made me infinite.* Sometimes it speaks from deep inside the presence. Sometimes the longed-for meeting is yet to come. #13 – *My whole life hopes for that meeting, but it has not happened yet.* There are ecstatic, triumphant moments, and there are times when the voice is "wearing out" its heart "with waiting and longing" (#41). The most beautiful of those is #47 – *This night and I are both nearly spent with waiting for him.* As Rumi says, *I am raw, and well-cooked, and burnt to a crisp.* (This is written on Rumi's tomb in Konya.) A human being can embody many different musics, and Rabindranath Tagore plays and sings a great many of them, in a lot of variations. It is good to remember here that Tagore is best-known in Bengal for his songs. He wrote over twenty-five hundred of them. "He has no equal," in that area, in the East or the West, said Satyajit Ray (Anthology, 354).

The great Tagore scholar-translators, Andrew Robinson and Krishna Dutta, say about Tagore's translations of himself, which the *Gitanjali* is, "The results were mainly mediocre, judged as English poetry" (Anthology, 354). I agree, and I hope to have raised them out of that deadly situation. I have condensed his language sometimes, and in other instances I have elaborated. With some poems, I changed very little. The wording of #62 is very similar to Tagore's. The ending of #51 is greatly altered with interpretations added regarding the meanings of the king's arrival, which are not there in the original. The eccentric, fifteen space indentation after the first line of each verse paragraph, I am not sure where that came from. I may be imitating something that I don't remember.

But as must be obvious to everyone, I have no scholarly credentials for working on these poems. I do not know much about the culture they come from, or anything about the language, Bengali. I have heard them sung in Bengali. I have heard a recording of Tagore singing them. He had a very beautiful voice. I just feel attracted to these poems, and somewhat attuned. I love the sense coming through them of an honest mysticism. That, of course, is also true of Rumi. That work prepared me for Tagore.

Five years after the *Gitanjali*, in 1917, Tagore, assisted by Evelyn Underhill, published an English translation of Kabir (the 14th century Hindu-Muslim poet), a favorite of Rabindranath's. Kabir's poems are in Hindi. I assume that Tagore worked from a Bengali translation, but I do not know whose. Robert Bly then in 1971 began to rework Tagore's translations to make *The Fish in the Sea Is Not Thirsty* (1972) and then in 1977 *The Kabir Book*, one of the most influential books of mystical poetry ever published. Bly describes his process, "I simply put a few of them (poems of Kabir in Tagore's English translations), whose interiors I had become especially fond of, into more contemporary language, to see what they might look like" (p. xix, *Kabir,* 2004). So something of a full circle is going on here. I have come back around to working on my mentor and friend's (Bly) mentor (Tagore's Kabir). It is very probable, of course, that Kabir knew Rumi's ecstatic poetry. Certainly Tagore did.

A Note on Gandhi and Tagore

These two so very different, and so very beautiful, embodiments of Indian culture in the early 20th century might be compared to Whitman and Lincoln, as two representative, and complementary, American archetypes from the mid-19th century. Gandhi and Tagore knew and respected each other, though they had some open differences. In May of 1933, Gandhi began a fast with a press statement. "Whether I survive the fast or not, is a matter of little moment. Without it I would in all probability have been useless for further service of Harijans (his work in eliminating the untouchables, the caste system), and for that matter, any other service." The intention of the fast is "to remove bitterness, to purify hearts, and to make it clear that the (non-cooperation) movement is wholly moral, to be prosecuted by wholly moral persons."

Tagore hears of Gandhi's fast and writes him a heartbreakingly honest letter: "I am trying clearly to find out the meaning of this last message of yours which is before the world today. As far as I can understand, the fast that you have started carries in it the idea of expiation for the sins of your countrymen . . . ..You ask others actively to devote their energy to extirpate the evil which smothers our national life and enjoin only upon yourself an extreme form of sacrifice which is of a passive character . . . . I cannot bear the sight of a sublimely noble career journeying toward a finality, which, to my mind, lacks a perfectly satisfying justification. The suffering that has been caused to me by the vow you have taken has compelled me to write you thus – With deepest pain and love, Rabindranath Tagore" (Anthology, 186).

When Gandhi finally broke his fast in Poona with a glass of orange juice, Rabindranath was there. He had taken a train across India from Calcutta. Before Gandhi drank the juice, Tagore was asked to sing Mahatma's (Tagore had given him this title) favorite song from the *Gitangali*. It was #39. Rabindranath began, but he had to improvise. He had forgotten the melody. That forgetting feels sublime.

Books you might want to look at:

*Rabindranath Tagore, An Anthology,* ed. Krishna Dutta and Andrew Robinson (New York: St. Martin's, 1997).
*Glimpses of Bengal, Selected from the Letters of Sir Rabindranath Tagore,* by Rabindrinath Tagore (Lexington, KY: Hard Press, 2010).
*Songs of Kabir,* trans. Rabindranath Tagore (New York: Macmillan, 1915).
*The Kabir Book,* trans. Robert Bly (Boston: Beacon Press, 1977).

# The Songs
## #1 - #103

#1

It pleases you that you have made me infinite,
    this fragile bowl you empty and empty again,
    and always fill with fresh life.

This reed flute you carry across the hills and play
    new lines of melody on, always new.

In your hands my heart loses the limits
    of its joy. No containing that.

Something is being said without using language.
    Gifts come and keep coming
    through these small hands.

Ages, still the pouring continues,
    and there is somehow room
    to hold the generosity.

You ask me to sing, my heart fills.
    I look in your face, and tears come.

All that is dissonant, harsh, in my life
    melts into a harmony.

Devotion, adoration, opens its wings over the ocean.

You enjoy the sound of my words.
    That is the only way
    I can reach your presence.

Only the wing-edge of my song
    can touch your feet.

In these poems I dissolve so totally
    I can call you friend
    who are my lord.

There are songs of yours
    that I listen to in silence.

Your music is inside the light of the sky,
    and inside the watertable as it breaks
    through rocks, and in the spring
    then that streams along.

My heart wants to find a voice
    that will let me join that music,
    but my speaking will not break into song.

You let me feel the threading motions of a music,
    but you do not give me the words
    that could disenthrall me from it.

Life inside my life, you are the purity
    that lives in me,

the deep touch of being throughout my body.
    You are the truth

that lit the clarity here in my mind.
    I protect

the inmost sacredness you are, this
    flowering of love.

It is my life's purpose to reveal you,
    whatever I do.

The strength I have to do
    that is your power moving in me.

Let me sit for a moment by your side.
    What I have been working on will wait.

When I am outside your presence, my heart is restless,
    and my work has no purpose.

Now summer has come with its light breathing sounds,
    and the courtly bees,

to this grove of trees where we sit with each other
    and silently sing this flood
    of freedom we live within.

Take this flower from where it grows.
    Lift it away with the pain of its
    breaking loose for your hand.

It may not be woven into a garland,
    but it will still be an offering.

Its color dim, its fragrance faint,
    let it be of some use to you,
    in time.

#7

My poem refuses all ornament,
    nothing decorative.

Only the naked simplicity of union,
    no elaboration, no poetic vanity.

I sit here at your feet. Let me make my life
    straight and empty

like the reed flute-cylinder
    so ready to fill with music.

A child wearing a prince's robes
    with jeweled chains around his neck

finds no pleasure in playing.
    He stays indoors, afraid to move.

Mother, it is not right to keep a child
    from playing on the ground,

that great health and gateway into the fair
    of all we have in common.

Fool, trying to carry yourself on your own shoulders.
    Beggar, come to beg at your own door.

There is a presence within all this. Surrender
    to that, and never look back.
    No regret.

Your desiring, with its breath, extinguishes the lamp.
    There is a more sacred love.

Accept the gift it brings. Only that blessing.
    Let the others go.

Here is your footstool with your feet at rest
    among the poor and the low.

When I try to bow to you there, I cannot
    reach to where you are

with the poorest, the low and the lost,
    those with no companions.

My heart, in its pride, cannot be with you
    there, with them.

Give up this fumbling with beads, this chanting
    in the dark, shut temple.

Who do you think you are worshiping in here
    all closed up?

Open your eyes. Open the doors and go outside.
    A man is plowing his field. A mason
    is breaking and laying stone for a path.

In rain and sunlight, covered with dust, the master
    of creation works inside our work.

Leave your meditation practice. Put away
    the incense and the essence-oil.

Get torn and exhausted in a day of physical work.
    You will find that God
    is working beside you.

This journey is long, and the way of it difficult.
    I came from a ray of sunlight

out into a wilderness of worlds,
    the stars and their planets.

The most remote course brings one
    to you.

In music, the most intricate training
    leads to utter simplicity.

A traveler must knock on every strange door
    to find his own.

Wander all the outer worlds
    to end up at your inmost shrine.

My eyes had to stray over and study
    a myriad landscapes

before I could shut them
    and say, *Here.*

The questioning cry, *Where?*
    has to flood and overflow

with tears to know the sudden,
    total truth, *I am.*

I have not sung the song I came here to sing.
    I have spent the time stringing
    and unstringing my instrument.

The words are not right. The truth of my time
    has not been said, only this
    deep longing in my heart.

The blossom has not opened in the wind.
    I have not seen his face,
    nor heard his voice.

Only the sound of his footsteps on the dirt road
    in front of my house.

I have spread the mat on the floor,
    making a place for him to sit,

but I have not lit the lamp or asked him in.
    I have lived my life hoping for this meeting,

but it has not happened yet.

Full of many kinds of desiring, my crying out
    remains confused and pitiful.

You save me with hard, definite refusals,
    and the strength of that mercy

has given my life a shape that makes me
    worthy of the great, simple gifts

you have given, unasked for: the sky, the light,
    this body, my mind.

These are what save me from excessive desire.
    I am sometimes lazy,

unfocused, distracted. Other times, I wake up
    and move with speed.

You coldly hide yourself in both cases,
    preparing me for your presence

by withholding it, and so saving me from what
    is most destructive: weak, uncertain love.

I am here to sing songs for you
      in this great hall where I have a corner seat.

I have no work, other than at intervals
      to break out in a useless new song.

Comes the call to silent worship in the midnight
      temple, ask me, my master,
      to stand there before you and sing.

When the morning light is tuning its gold harp,
      command my presence
      to come into yours.

I have been invited to the world's great gathering
      to play my instrument and sing.

I have been blessed by
      what my eyes have seen, what my ears have heard.

At this feast I have done all that I could. Is it time now
      for me to go in and see your face
      and offer you my silence?

I am waiting for love, only that.
    Your presence.

That is why it is so late and why
    there are so many things
    I have not done.

They come with their rules, their social
    conventions, to put limits on me.

I can avoid those. I get away. I will give myself,
    finally and only, to love.

People are right to call me reckless.
    It is true that I do not care.

The market day is over. The busy ones have come
    expecting something from me.

They have gone away angry, and I am still waiting,
    as I have always been,
    for a love to surrender into.

Cloud-masses over cloud layer, darkening.
    Why do you keep me waiting
    outside, alone?

In the noon work-hour I am with the world,
    but in this rain, this louring light,
    I look only for you.

If you do not show me your face,
    how will I get through these hours,

with my heart so weeping and restless
    in the fitful wind?

#19

If I hear no words from you, I accept the silence
        and wait as the night does in its star-vigil,
        head bent low, patient.

Morning will come, with your voice
        in the pouring light.

Words will lift again from their birdnests,
        and from me, as song does
        from wildflowers in the woods.

On the day when the lotus opened,
　　my mind was elsewhere,

unaware what had happened,
　　my basket empty.

Only, several times during the day,
　　sadness came over me,

and I was startled, as from a dream,
　　by a fragrance in the wind,

a vague, tender longing as though
　　of the summer for itself.

I did not know that what was so near
　　was in fact *inside* me.

A perfect sweetness had bloomed
　　inside my heart.

#21

I must set out on the ocean.
     The shoreland has grown stale.

Spring has flowered and left. I wait here
     among dead discolored shapes,

with wave-voices urging me to start out,
     and pieces of yellow fallen
     on the forest path.

What emptiness are you staring into?
     Do you not hear the ache and the thrill
     of song in the air
     calling you to begin again?

#22

Walking silently this dark rain-soaked July,
  no one sees you.

Morning has closed its eyes,
  a cloth drawn across the blue.

No sound in the forest. Doors are shut
  on every house.

You are alone out walking, my friend.
  Do not pass by here like a dream.

The gate to my house is open.

Night-storm groaning like someone in love.
    Several times I open

my door to look out in the darkness for you.
    I see nothing.

By some edge of ink-black slough, in some
    labyrinth of pathways through the woods,

you are finding a way toward me,
    are you not?

## #24

Day over, birds quiet, the wind dies down.
    Darkness wraps the earth in sleep.

Lotus petals close. His sack is empty
    before the traveler is through
    with traveling.

Exhausted, torn, covered with grime.
    Wash away the shame of poverty.

Renew him like a flower in the shelter
    of kindness, your night.

Let me give up in the night to sleep,
    to trust this tiredness.

Do not let me force myself to do
    some weary form of praising.

Draw over the night-cover and make
    these exhausted eyes close
    to let fresh waking come,
    a new, never-felt, gladness.

#26

You came and sat by my bed, but I did not wake.
 You came in the still part of night
 with music in your hands.

I was dreaming the songs you sang,
 but I did not wake.

Why do I not see the one
 who breathes in my sleep?

Light, there must be more light,
      the kind that comes from intense living.

There is a lamp, but it has no flame inside.
      Do not let my heart be like that.

Death is far better than a lamp
      with no lambent fire inside.

Grief comes to the door with a message.
      *Your lord is awake and calling for you.*

Constant rain, thick overcast.
      A lightning flash makes the dark deeper.

But a music calls me out
      into the stone-black night.

Only a lit lamp will carry us through this,
      a soul that burns with longing.

What holds me is a stubbornness.
    When I try to break with it,
    heartache comes.

All I want is to be free, but I feel ashamed
    when I hope for that.

This friendship is the real wealth,
    but I refuse to sweep up and throw away
    the strands of tinsel on the floor of my room.

I hate this heavy shroud that covers me,
    but also I hug it close.

Debt, failure, secret shame. These keep me
    from moving, but when I pray for release,
    I am afraid that what I ask for
    may be given.

The one inside my name weeps
    in the dungeon I have built.

So diligently working, with small plastering
    repair, sand and dust and water,

I have been busy with this name-life,
    this prison wall-work,
      forgetting the being I am.

I start out alone to meet you. Someone
    is following. I turn aside
      to throw him off. It doesn't work.

He adds insistent pressure to my voice, and swagger
    to my stride. More dust rises.

He is my ego, the small selfish self, who feels
    no shame, but I am ashamed
      to come to you in his company.

Who bound you this way? *My master did this.*
  *I thought I could acquire more wealth*
  *and power than anyone.*

*I kept money that was due my king.*
  *A sleep came over.*

*I slept in his bed and woke up locked*
  *in my own treasury.*

Prisoner, tell me again. Who made these chains?
  *I made them unbreakable,*
  *with cruel strong strokes on the anvil.*

*When the work was complete, I tested the links,*
  *found they were holding me.*

Those who love me in this world try in many ways
    to keep me safe and steady.

You, with your love that is greater than theirs,
    want me *free.*

Those who want me secure are always nearby.
    They will not leave me alone,
    but days pass when I do not see you.

The truth is: Even if I do not talk with you,
    or keep you in my heart, your love
    is still closeby waiting for my love.

In the morning light they come to my house
      and say, *We shall only need*
      *your smallest room, nothing else.*

*We are here to help you worship your God*
      *and will only accept our share*
      *of the grace that comes.*

They sit quietly on the floor in a corner.
      But in the dark middle of the night

I find they have broken into my most sacred place
      and taken everything off the altar.

Of me, let only that little be left
    that lets me say your name.

Of my will, only that that feels you all around,
    and moves with love toward you.

Let only such a little be left
    that I could never hide inside it.

Let my only binding be what holds me
    in your will, your love.

Into a mind without fear,
      not compartmented by domestic walls,

where words come from a true depth,
      where energy reaches toward perfection,

where clarity has not sunk down in the sands of habit,
      where intelligence lifts out on the sky,

let this world wake, my father,
      into a widening field of thought and action.

Cut the roots of stinginess in my heart.

Give me the strength of lightness
    in both elation and depression.

Let my loving be helpful.

Do not let me avoid helping the poor
    or bow to the insolence of the powerful.

Help me stay undistracted
    by what does not matter.

Strike down in these ways,
    and let my strength be your strength.

I thought my traveling was over,
       that my creative powers were at an end,
       provisions exhausted.

Silence began to feel like good shelter.

But now your will stirs in me again.
       As language fades from the voice,
       a new music springs in the heart.

One path ends. Another countryside
       reveals itself.

That I long only for you, my heart keeps repeating.
    My other desirings are vacant at the core.

As night keeps hidden in itself an impulse toward light,
    so in the depth of my unconscious
    lives a crying-out.

A thunderstorm is looking for peace
    when it strikes down with sudden wildness,

so my resistance to your love says,
    with its pushing away, *you, you.*

When my heart is dry and impenetrable,
    rain down your grace.

When I am dull and without energy,
    send song through me.

When the surrounding noise overwhelms,
    come with your silence and rest.

When I am crouched in a backroom corner
    like a homeless beggar,

break open the door and take me into
    the majesty of friendship.

When desire blinds me with illusion,
    wake me up with thunder
    and the lit lamp of the soul.

No rain for days. My God. Sky fiercely
    empty, no thinnest cloud,
      not the hint of a shower in my heart.

I pray for storm, a death-sky lightning-lash
    from horizon to horizon inside me.

Call back this silent heat into yourself,
    this keen self-cruelty.

Bend low with dense raincloud like the compassion
    of a mother's tenderness
    on the day of the father's anger.

Are you somewhere behind these others, my lover,
    standing in shadow?

I wait here by the road with my flower-offerings.
    People come and take the flowers,

one by one. Now my basket is empty. Morning,
    noon, evening. The men going home

smile at me. I sit like a young beggar maid,
    dropping my eyes, saying nothing.

My love, should I tell them that you promised me
    you would come, that this waiting
    and this poverty are my dowry?

With my secret, I sit in the grass and imagine
    the glory of your coming,
    light, and gold pennants flying.

You will lift me onto the seat beside you.
    The roadside gossips cannot believe. . ..

This trembling girl like a wall vine in the breeze.
    Still no noise of wheels.

Are you there in the shadow behind the crowd?
    Am I here wearing out my heart
    with waiting and longing?

Early in the day there was a feeling that you and I
    would sail out in a boat
    on a pilgrimage to nowhere on a shoreless ocean.

My poems would come to us there as free
    as the waves, and as wordless as waves.

Is it time now for that setting out,
    or is there more to do here?

With evening shore birds flying to their nests
    can we not like the sunset
    vanish with them into the night?

There was a time when I was not always
    waiting for your presence.

You came to me anyway, a king disguised
    as a commoner, and pressed your signet ring
    on my small moment, eternity imprinting time.

I look back now and see so clearly
    how you did not turn away
    from my childhood playing,
    those forgotten days.

You were with me there in the backyard,
    as you are with me now
    in the great spaces between stars.

# #44

This is my deep delight, to wait and watch beside the road.
    Shadow chasing light. Cold rain
    coming to the end of summer.

Sky-messengers arrive, clouds. In the sweet breeze
    of their passing my heart feels
    completely alive.

I sit on my doorstep from dawn to dusk.
    I know the sudden moment of seeing will come.

Meanwhile, I smile and sing here alone. Meanwhile, in the air
    a perfume of possibility.

Have you heard the sound of someone's footsteps
     coming, every day, closer,

through every age, in each moment,
     moving nearer?

I have composed many songs with different words
     and emotions. Each note is saying,
     *He is coming.*

The fragrant April forest, thick rain on a July night,
     the rolling wheels of its thunder,
     everything says the same.

In grief after grief, I feel the pressure of his foot
     on the ground. My joy
     is the gold light he walks inside.

I have felt you always moving near.
    But from what distant time,
    I do not know.

The sun and the stars reveal you.

Morning and evening your messenger
    speaks secretly inside my heart.

Now a trembling all through me today,
    a joy, as though my time

were almost over, with your presence
    lightly carried in the air.

This night and I are both nearly spent
    with waiting for him.

I am afraid that he will come in the morning,
    when I am in my deepest first sleep.

Friends, leave the way open.
    Do not prevent him, and if

his footsteps do not wake me, I pray let
    nothing else do so,

not the birds nor the wind or the great marketplace
    of morning light.

Keep me inside you, precious sleep.
    Let only his touch, the light of his smile,

be firstlight for me. Let my awakened soul
    be held in his glance.

Let my return to self be immediate and the same
    as my return to him.

Morning silence. The smooth sea of it ripples into birdsong.
    Flowers beside the road, a deep gold
    break in the cloudbank.

We are busy beginning our day. We barely notice.
    We do not sing or play instruments.

We do not go to market with things we have made,
    to barter. We do not speak to anyone,

or smile. We speed up to make better time.
    Noon. Doves coo in the shade. Dead leaves
    spin down. Shepherd boy asleep under the banyan.

I stretch out in the grass by the creek. My friends laugh
    at my tiredness and hurry by,
    needing no rest, into the blue haze.

I honor their journey through strange cities
    that I will never see.

Their mockery almost got me up, back on the road,
    but not. Lying back

in glad humiliation, sun-threaded green air
    spreading through my psyche,

I forget why I ever set out. I surrender my mind again
    to shadow and song and sleep.

Now I wake to see you flooding into me your smile.

I had so wrongly thought the way was long
    and difficult, the one
    that reaches into your presence.

#49

You came down from your throne
    to the door of my house.

Now you are standing on my threshold.
    You heard a small song rising
    from this corner and came.

Among all the music-masters in your hall
    you heard a strain that you liked
    mingling with the great music of the world,
    something of mine.

You bring a single wildflower to give to me
    as I give this to you.

I am begging door to door through the village
      when I see your sun-chariot in the distance
      like a dream coming nearer,

right to where I stand. I feel everything changing,
      great wealth about to rain down.
      Finally, some good luck.

Then you hold out your right hand.
      "What will you give me?"

*Some kind of royal joke?* I think.
      I don't know what to do.

I feel in my bag, find a tiny corn grain,
      and put it in your hand.

At the end of the day I empty out on the floor
      the pitiful pickings of a beggar's day.

Among the worthless trash, a kernel of pure gold
      exactly the size of the bit of corn.

I weep. I should have had the expanse of heart
      to give you everything, my soul,
      every part of my being alive.

Night darkens. We have done all we can this day.
    The last traveler has been lodged.
    The village gate shut.

Someone says, "The king is coming."
    We laugh. "Impossible."

We douse the lamps and lie down.
    A knocking sound. A messenger?
    Only the wind.

Later in the dead middle of night, another sound.
    Thunder, surely.

A rumbling of great wheels. We speak
    from sleep, the clouds.

In the pre-dawn a definite drum.
    Someone says, "The king's flag!"

We dress quickly in the dark. *We need torches,*
    *flowers, a throne.*

Hopeless. We must welcome him with what we have,
    which is nothing,
    empty hands, bare rooms.

The darkness shudders with lightning. Open the doors.
    Sound the conch shells.

We bring out a piece of torn mat and lay it down
    in the courtyard.

The king of the night storm, the king of our fear
    of not being ready, has come.

A lover, the woman, is musing in the morning
    after her lord, the beloved, has gone.

*I wish I had asked for the rose wreath*
    *around your neck. I did not dare to.*

*Here now is only a stray petal on the floor.*
    *Have you left me some token of your love,*
    *a flower, spices, a vase of perfumed water?*

*No. You have left your sword, like a living flame.*

With the young light of morning on the empty bed,
    a bird at the window asks,
    "What has he given you?"

*I wonder about this gift, too heavy to carry.*
    *Nowhere to hide it. It hurts, against me.*

*You have given me death as a friend to walk with.*
    *But no fear, nothing can bind me*

*now I have this keen, swift discernment. No more*
    *weeping and waiting.*

*The lord of my heart wants no decoration,*
    *nothing flirtatious, nothing coy.*

*No doll clothes nonsense.*
    *I have my sword.*

The bracelet of your stars has cunning workmanship:
    the differently-colored jewels – emerald,
    yellow sapphire, jade, ruby.

But your sword is more beautiful to me: a lightning-curve
    of outspread wings like a Vishnu bird
    poised against the flame of sunset,

in a trembling last response, the ecstasy of its pain.
    Earthly senses burn up in one fierce flash.

Your inlaid wrist ornament has appeal, but the thunder-sword
    is a continually growing beauty,
    terrible both to see and to remember.

#54

I did not ask you for anything. I never told you my name.
    When you left, I was silent by the well
    in the slant tree-shadow.

The women with their brown clay pitchers
    filled to the brim were walking away.

They call back to me, *Come with us.*
    *It is almost noon.*

Lost in my musing, I do not answer.
    Nor do I hear you return,

your voice tired, your eyes sad.
    *I am a thirsty traveler.*

I rouse from my daydreaming and pour water
    into your palms joined together for a bowl.

Leaves overhead, cuckoo calling from the dark,
    the *babla* flower's scent.

You ask my name. Why would you want to know that?
    Because I once gave you water?

That is such a dear memory.
    It folds me in its sweetness.

Late morning now, birdsong diminishing,
    *neem* leaves rubbing against each other.

In that sound I sit back
    in a vague remembering.

Tiredness in your heart, sleep
    closing the eyes.

Have you not heard? A majestic flower
    has opened among the thorns.

It is time to wake. My friend sits alone
    at the end of a stony path.

Do not deceive him. So noon is troubled
    in the heat,

and sand spreads its robe of thirst
    over our solitude.

Remember the deep joy in your heart,
    and how the harp of the road

sounds with each footstep
    the sweet music of your pain.

#56

It has happened this way. Your joy is so full
  in me. If I were not,
  how could your love take form?

You have taken me as your partner, with your delight
  living in my heart as playfulness.

Your will continuously takes
  different shapes in my life.

Your love has lost itself in my loving. The perfection
  of this union is the great beauty I feel all around me.

Light. There is a light in the center of my heart,
    and at the core of existence.

The same light that fills the world fills me,
    eye-kissing light.

The same light that strikes lightning opens the wind
    in a wild laughter moving across.

Butterflies lift their sails on a sea of this light.
    Lily and jasmine ride the crest of its waves.

Scattered gold on the clouds, this joy is a river
    of light, a great gladness above us
    flooding over its banks.

Let all the strands of joy mix
    in the music of my last poem:

the joy that lets the ground flow over itself
    in the form of ever-lengthening grasses,

the one that dances with these daft twin
    brothers, life and death,

the one that comes in on the storm
    shaking everyone awake with its laughter.

Also the joy that sits in tears on the splayed open
    red lotus of pain.

And finally the joy that throws everything it has
    into the dust, under the dust,
    and knows not one word.

The golden light in the leaves is nothing but your love,
  these clouds idling across,
   this breeze on my forehead.

The morning light that floods my eyes
  is what you are saying to me,
   with your face bending to look into mine.

My heart is touching your feet.

When children meet on the beach, the beach is endless.
    Above them, a motionless sky.

The ocean beside them, restless, hilarious. When children
    shout to each other on the beach,

eternity is in the motions of their feet,
    and in their hands that build sand-houses
    and gather shells.

A dead leaf is a boat to float on seawater.

The children on the sandy edge do not know
    how to swim or how to cast nets.

They make piles of pebbles. Then they scatter them.
    They do not look for anything valuable.

The pearl divers are doing that,
    and the merchant ships.

The ocean smiles in the sheen on the sand
    and sings a meaningless death-ballad.

Old mother rocking, the sea plays
    with her grandchildren.

On this beach where children meet
    nothing is known of shipwreck
    or of being lost in a storm.

Death is everywhere out on the ocean,
    but on this beach
    there is only a meeting of children,

their play, and world within world.

A baby's eyelid flutters in sleep.
    Does anyone know where that comes from?

Yes. There is a village in the forest
    lit only with lightning bugs.

Two rosebuds there share an enchantment
    with the baby. They come to kiss
    the sleeping eyelids, invisibly.

A smile plays on a sleeping baby's lips.
    Do we know where that comes from?

Yes. A new crescent moon touches the edge
    of an autumn cloud just as it is vanishing,
    as dew is forming in the grass.

That washed moment makes the baby smile.

The softness of the baby's skin, does anyone know
    where it was before? Yes.

When the mother was a young girl, something
    was hidden in the mystery of her silence
    and in the ways of her young loving.

*That is what blooms in the freshness*
    *on the baby's skin.*

When I bring my child colorful toys,
    I understand why there is a play
    of color on clouds and water,
    and why the flowers are here.

When I sing to make you dance,
    I hear leaf-music closer, and I know
    why the waves sing a chorus
    into the listening shore. When I sing
    to make you dance.

When I bring sweetness to your hungry hands,
    my child, I know

why there is honey in the flower's cup,
    why fruits fill secretly with juice.

When I kiss your face to make you smile,
    my darling, I know more clearly

what pleasure is in the morning sky, that light,
    and what delight the wind
    in summer brings my body.
    When I kiss you to make you smile.

You bring me new friends.
      You sit me down in homes that are not my own.

You make the distant near and the stranger
      my companion.

I feel uneasy when I leave my usual shelter.
      I forget that the old is inside the new,
      and that you are there as well.

Through this world and others, through birthing
      and dying, you are my one traveling companion.

You link me with joy to the unfamiliar. With you
      there is nothing foreign, no shut door.

I have a prayer. May I never lose this feeling
      of your whole touch, your oneness,
      in the midst of the false sensation
      of the many.

My house is dark and empty. On the sloping riverbank
    among the tall grasses I ask
    where she is going with her lamp.

You should bring your light into my house.
    *I come here to float my lamp*
    *on the river surface in the dusk.*

So I stand in the tall grass watching her lamp
    drift vaguely on the tide.

In the deeper night I invite her in again.
    Her dark eyes study my face.

*I have dedicated my lamp to the sky.*
    And I watch her tiny light
    burning against the black.

At midnight I ask a third time why she keeps
    her lamp so near her heart.

My house is lonesome for lamplight.
    Can you lend me yours?

*This lamp is meant to join*
    *with the great carnival of lights.*

I watch her light get uselessly lost
    among a hundred others.

I ask my God, "Would you like to drink
    from this overflowing of mine?

"Source of poetry, is it your delight
    to see creation through my eyes,

"to stand in the doorway of my ears and listen
    to your own harmonies?

"Your world weaves words inside me.
    Your joy puts music in those words.

"You give yourself to me in love,
    and you feel then your own wholeness,
    your tenderness, in me."

She who stays hidden in my deep being,
    she who has never seen the morning,
    or the twilight,

she will be my last gift to you,
    folded inside my final poem.

Though words cannot reach the one I have taken
    around from country to country inside
    the growing and the decay of this body-life.

Every thought and action, every dream
    and dreamlessness fills with that one
    who remains unreachable.

Many come and ask, but no face has yet seen
    the one who waits for you
    to recognize her.

You are the sky *and* the nest,
    the nest where you wrap yourself around
    with color and sound and fragrance.

The nest is how you love.

Morning comes with a basket in her right hand
    distributing beauty.

Evening comes alone over the hillside meadow,
    empty now of animals, carrying cool cupfuls
    of rest in her gold pitcher.

Now there is this clear, opening, sky
    for the soul to take flight in, to explore.

This white radiance has no day or night, no form, no color,
    and not a sign of a word.

We are connected by a ray of light. It comes from you
      and stays by my door all day.

In the evening it carries back to you clouds
      made of my songs, my breathing sadness.

You wrap yourself with the mists of that cloud-robe.
      You turn within it making innumerable shapes,
      astonishing color-mixings,
      always changing the tone and the light.

So momentary and tender and fragile and darkening –
      that is why you love it so,
      and why you let it cover, briefly,
      your serene brilliance
      with its sentimental shadowplay.

The same living stream that runs in my veins
    runs in the wild rhythms of the world.

It breaks through the ground into grassblades,
    into waves of flowers and lifting leaf-branches,

ebbing out and back in with the ocean tides of birthing
    and dying, night and day.

My arms and legs are made glorious
    with the passage of time,
    in the throb-dance of blood,
    the fullness I feel this moment.

Is it beyond you to be part of this furious rush
      of being alive,

the joy and the speed of being broken
      apart, lost and afraid?

Everything whirls about in the inexorable music
      of the seasons, a blur of color.
      Melodies mix, confusing fragrances.

A waterfalling, drowning excitement is enjoying
      itself, the giving up and dying.

Every moment death, but nothing stops,
      or looks back.

It scatters and splashes on its restless dance.
      Are you inside this?

#71

When I make much of myself, you call it *maya*.
     I call it my life, as I turn in your radiance
     casting colored shadows.

You divide yourself from yourself.
     I am that dividedness.
     I am your defeated part.

The screen you put up is being painted
     with a big brush of night-and-day.
     It is swarming with figures.

You are seated behind the screen on a throne
     made only of curving lines,
     no straightness.

A living pageant of you and me spreads across the sky.
     The air is vibrant with music.

Ages of the world go by, and all that happens
     is this hiding and uncovering
     of you and me.

You are the inward being
    who wakes me with your touch.

You put mystery inside my eyes
    and joy in the musical pleasure and pain
    that come through my heart.

You weave the web of what appears,
    what comes and goes,

on a green field turning bluish, flecks
    of gold and silver.

I reach to touch your feet. I dissolve.
    You move within many guises
    with many names, disappointment,
    a sudden elation.

#73

I do not find freedom in renouncing,
    rather in being tangled with delight.

Bondage to that is my deliverance.
    Every day you pour fresh wine,
    always to the brim.

I light a hundred different lamps for your altar,
    and I will not shut the doors of my senses.

Sight and hearing, touch and taste,
    are also ways into you.

For me, illusion burns through to illumination,
    and all my desiring ripens
    into the fruit of love.

With daylight leaving, shadow covers the ground.
    It is time for me to go to the stream
    and fill my pitcher.

The evening air eager over the sad flow-music of the creek
    calls me out into itself.

No one else is on the path. A slight wind
    ripples across the river surface.

I may not go back home. I don't know.

Who might I meet out here
    by chance? In his boat by the fording place a man
    is playing his lute.

What you give is everything we need,
    yet it streams back to you unchanged,

as riverwater does its work coming down
    through the fields and the small towns,
    always hoping to wash your feet.

A flower sweetens the garden air, wanting at last
    to serve as an offering to you.

Such worship takes nothing away from the world.

People derive many meanings from poems.
    All of them lead into your presence.

Day after day, lord of all the worlds, is this how it is,
    that I shall stand with folded hands facing you?

In solitude and silence shall I stand
    humbly under the sky?

Among the busy, tumultuous crowds of people
    working and going to work,

shall I stand here looking at you
    with my hands folded?

And when my time is done, my work over, lord of my life,
    shall I stand alone and speechless in front of you
    face to face with my hands folded?

I call you *God* and move back a little,
    rather than come closer.

Bowing to touch your feet,
    I address you as *father.*

If I could acknowledge you as my friend,
    I could travel side by side with you,
    heart inside heart.

You are a brother among my other brothers,
    but I do not share my earnings with them,
    and so not with you.

In pleasure and pain I do not stand with others,
    and so I remain separate from you.

I avoid giving up my life and so do not dive
    into the great rushing river
    of being alive inside you.

When the createdness was new, the stars
    from their first radiance sang in the assembly,
    *Ah perfection, pure joy!*

Then someone said suddenly, *There has been a break*
    *in the chain of light. One star lost.*

A gold harp string snapped. The singing stopped.
    *That lost star was the best of us.*

The searching began from that day. A grief-cry
    goes up that the universe
    has lost its deep-felt well-being.

Now only sometimes in the middle of the silence of night
    do some of them whisper among themselves,

*Nothing has been lost really. The perfection*
    *is unbroken still.*

If I am not to meet you in this life,
    let me carry the pain of that not happening
    in every moment, waking or dreaming.

In the crowded market, with my hands full of profits,
    let me feel the emptiness.

When I rest beside the road, let me remember
    the long journey ahead.

when in the middle of flute music
    and laughter in my own house,

let me be continuously aware
    of how I have not invited you
    to this gathering.

I feel like a piece of autumn cloud
      the sun has not yet evaporated
      into itself, its light.

Is this the way you want the months and the years
      of my separation from you to be?

Is this how you are playing with me, you sun, my lord
      and friend? Then spread color over this
      emptiness-about-to-disappear,

a thin gold light on wanton gauze. When the playing ends,
      maybe I will dissolve in your nightdark,
      maybe in the clear of some white morning.

## #81

I weep over the time wasted, idling.
      But no moment is lost.

In the heart of existence growth and nourishment
      are still going on.

Seeds break open, begin to sprout, bud loosens
      to blossom, flower condenses to fruit.

As I sleep late into the afternoon,
      work is thriving in the garden.

I wake to find it thick with flowers,
      in never-imagined variations.

For you there is no counting minutes.
    Days and nights bloom and pass
    in your eternity of waiting.

Centuries are needed to perfect the color and design
    of a single wildflower.

We, on the other hand, scramble for more time,
    too poor to be late.

We argue and grab for chances. I give my time
    to any insistent man who claims to own it.

Your altar stays empty.

I hurry to make it before your gate shuts.
    Then I learn there is still more time.

Mother, each grief is a pearl around your neck.
    The constellations, anklets of light.

Whatever blessings we have come from you,
    as do the blessings withheld.

Only this grieving sadness is my own.

When I finally bring this to you,
    you will give your deepest grace.

The feel of being separate spreads through the world
    and shapes appear in the sky because of that.

A grief of being apart stares in silence at the stars,
    and a song-like rainy fluttering
    moves in the leaves of July.

This pain deepens our love and our desire.

Inside our human homes the suffering of this knowing
    flows in these lyrics moving through me.

When the warriors first came out from
    their master's hall,

they had no armor and no arms.
    Where was their power?

They looked helpless, and the arrows
    rained down.

As they marched back in to their master's hall,
    they had hidden their power again.

They had dropped their swords somewhere,
    their bows and their arrows.

Peace was on their brows. Whatever
    they had done in their lives,

all that was left behind, as they walked back in
    again to their master's hall.

Death, your messenger is at my door.
    He has crossed the unknowable night sea
    and arrived here with word from you.

I open my gate and bow to him, in tears.
    I place the gift of my heart at his feet.

He will go back with his errand done,
    leaving a dark shadow on my morning.

All that's left here now is this desolate self,
    which I will bring soon enough
    as a last offering for you.

I search the corners of my room. She is not here.
    My house is so small that when someone
    is gone, she cannot be brought back.

But your mansion is infinite. She must be
    somewhere in there.

This gold evening sky-canopy
    is the edge of eternity, the place
    where we meet,

where nothing can disappear, no joy, no memory
    of a face seen through tears.

Dip my emptiness into this ocean. Let me feel again
    her lost dear human touch
    in the whole vastness of the universe.

Your presence is felt in the temple ruin,
        in the broken strings of the vina,
        in the bells that do not ring for evening prayer.

In air so still and silent, you are a desolation,
        a spring breeze through the toppled stone.
        Flowers *not* brought.

In the firelight evening a worshiper looks for you,
        longing and wandering, still refused,
        in the empty, wall-less rooms.

Old festival days pass in silence.

Intricate new images are built elsewhere,
        have their day, and leave the scene.

You remain in the barren sanctuary, unworshiped.
        Eternal neglect.

What wants to come through me now
    are bits of whispering, your pleasure.

No more declarative sentences, nothing loud
    or definite. Song-murmur.

While everyone is busy in the market,
    I take off, I and the midday bees,
    lazing, called outside to play,

where the garden is
    flowering early, out of season,
    and I am drawn to my friend out
    wanderlooking, sing-saying
    some almost-nothing.

On the day when death comes to your door,
    what will you give him?

I will give my autumn afternoons, summer nights,
    the gleanings from my harvest,
    all I have ever earned.

When I answer that knocking, I will bring
    my whole life, the full bowl
    of everything I lived through and am.

#91

My death comes to speak with me.
    I have been waiting for this.

As I look in those eyes, your eyes,
    everything in my life will be yours,

the bridegroom's flowers woven in a garland.

Now the bride leaves her home to meet her lord.
    In the solitude of night they will be alone.

I know the day is coming when I will not see this world,
    and silence, like a curtain, comes across.

Stars will still rise. Morning will brighten, and the tides still
    come in with their pleasure and pain.

When I remember this end of my moments,
    when I see by death-light,
    each trivial event becomes rare.

Whatever I have longed for, and whatever I have gotten,
    none of those matter.

What I want now is what I did not want before,
    what I overlooked.

I have seen the signal. Say goodbye, my friends.
    I give back my house keys
    and all claim to any possessions.

All I ask is a few last kind words,
    an answering bow.

We were good neighbors. I received from you
    much more than I gave.

Daylight is here. The lamp that lit my corner
    is out. A lifted arm. I am ready.

## #94

Wish me luck on this journey, starting out as I am
    in the flushed sky of dawn, on a beautiful path.

I take nothing with me, just empty hands,
    an empty, expectant heart.

A garland of wedding flowers around my neck,
    not the red-brown traveler's dustcoat.

There are definite dangers to face,
    but I have no fear.

By the time the evening star comes out,
    I will be where I can hear the aching
    flute notes of the king's twilight gate-song.

When I crossed over into this life,
    I was not conscious of a threshold.

What was it made me open out into this wide midnight
    like a flower in the woods?

Morning light, and I know now that I am not a stranger here,
    that the unknowable, the power that has no name and no form,
    is holding me in its arms as my very own mother.

When I die, that same unknowable will appear familiar.
    Because I love this life so much, I will love death too.

A child cries out when its mother lifts it away from the right breast,
    only then to find again what it loves in the left.

When I go from this place, let my last sentence be
      that what I have seen here is beyond describing.

I have tasted a secret honey inside the lotus,
      and that has expanded into an ocean of light.

I have felt such blessing. Let that be what I say
      when I am leaving.

This is a theatre of infinite playing.
      I have played many parts.

I have caught sight of and felt the touch
      of one beyond touch.

If the end of this is the very end, I accept that.
      Let gratitude be what is felt
      in what I say then.

Playing with you, I never thought to ask
    who you were.

No fear, no shyness, my life was
    boisterous spontaneity.

You called me early from sleep and sent me running
    from field to wood to stream to another field.

I never thought about the meaning of the songs
    you sang inside me.

My voice already knew the music
    and my heart the right rhythm.

That playing time is over now. This vision comes:
    of the world bowing to touch your feet,
    then standing in awe
    for the silent nightsky, and all the stars.

I give you the flowers of my surrender.
    I never thought I would escape
    without surrendering.

Whatever I am proud of must open out in pain,
    like my hollow heart with its reed sound.

The stone must melt in tears and let the hundred-petaled lotus
    reveal the honey of its center.

Now the sky's blue eye calls me into silence,
    and you give your final gift,
    which is nothing whatever,
    complete emptiness.

When I give up control of my life,
    it goes to you.

What needs to be done will instantly
    be done with no effort.

It is the heart's surrender to sit still,
    blessedly content
    with wherever this is.

Every lamp has been blown out by the wind.
    I shall not try to re-light them.

I wait in this dark with a mat spread out
    on the floor beside me.

Whenever you want to,
    please come sit with me.

I dive deep into the ocean of form,
      looking for the perfect spirit-pearl.

No more sailing one harbor to another
      in this battered boat. I used to love the sport
      of being thrown about on the waves.

Now I want eternity, to tune my instrument to that,
      the stringed instrument of my life.

Let a new music rise in the audience hall,
      something like a sob, or an inbreath gasp.

I will eventually lay this instrument down
      at the feet of silence.

## #101

I have tried to find you with poetry.
    Song led me door to door.

With poems I have found ways to touch
    and know the world.

Everything I have ever found, the secret paths,
    the star on the horizon,

I was guided to by poems. Into the mystery of pleasure,
    into the mystery of grief.

It is evening now at the end of my traveling.
    What is this astonishing gate
    they have brought me to?

#102

I bragged in company that I have known you. People see your image in what I have drawn.

They come to ask, *Who is he?*
        I don't know what to say. I have no words.
        They go away. You sit there smiling.

I put stories of you into poems that will last for centuries.
        A secret part of you flows out of me.

They come again. *Say more about the meanings.*
        Again I shrug. *No one can say much.*

They ridicule my life and leave.
        You sit there with your smile.

In one recognition, one sentence,
    let all my senses spread out to touch this world
    that bows at your feet.

Like a July raincloud heavy and low with unshed showers,
    let my intelligence offer what it must
    in one salutation at your door.

Let every song I ever worked on
    gather their diverse strands and flow
    as one motion to your sea of silence.

Like a flock of homesick cranes flying at night,
    and all day too, back

to a mountain nest, let my life become one
    wing-wave going home into you.

# Four Poems from The Crescent Moon

## The Astronomer

As a boy I said to my father, "When the round full moon gets
    caught in the branches of the *kadam*-tree,
      why couldn't somebody catch it?"
He said, "Silly child, the moon is so far from us!
    No one can catch it."
I told him, "When mother looks down at us playing from her
    window, is she far away?"
He said, "Where would you find a net big enough
    to catch the moon?"
I said, "You could catch it in your hands."
Father said, "If the moon came closer,
    you would see how big it is."
I said, "That's the nonsense you've been taught at school.
    When mother bends her face close,
      do you think she's getting bigger?"
Father, "Silly child."

## The Champak Flower

Imagine if I became a champak flower.
Just for fun, growing high up on that tree, in the wind.
I would open my petals and watch you working.
You would call to me, "Where are you?"
I would laugh and keep quiet.
Then, after your bath, with your hair wet on your shoulders,
     you would walk through the shadow of this champak
     tree, to the little courtyard where you say your prayers.
You would notice the sweet flower-scent,
     not knowing that it came from me.
Then after the noon meal, as you sat in the window reading
     the Ramayana, I would cause my tiny shadow
     to fall across your book, just at the place
     you were reading.
Then at night, when you go to the cowshed with your lamp,
     I would suddenly drop down
     to the ground again,
     and be your little child.
"Where have you been?"
"What have you been doing?"
"I will not tell you, mother."
"That's how we will be talking then."

## Authorship

You say that father writes a lot of books,
    but I don't understand what he is saying in them.
"All evening he was reading to you. Did you understand?"
"Mother, I love the stories that you tell us.
    Why can't father write like that?"
Did he never hear stories from his mother?
Fairytales of giants and princesses?
Has he forgotten those?
Sometimes in the night when you have run his bath,
    he forgets, and you have to call and call.
You keep his food warm, but he does not come.
He forgets and goes back to his writing.
Always writing and writing. What fun is that?
But when I take up his pen and make marks, a,b,c,d,e,f,g,h,i,
    you get cross and say I'm being bad.
He makes black marks, wasting both sides
    of many sheets of paper. You say nothing.
I take one sheet to make a boat. You say I'm wasting time.
What about all those sheets of paper
    he scribbles on to make his books?
He makes black marks all over both sides!

## My Song

My child, this song will hold you in its arms like music.
It will kiss you on your forehead like a blessing.
When you are sitting alone, it will whisper in your ear.
In a crowd of noisy people it will make a place of quietness
      around you.
It will give wings to your dreams.
They will fly you to unknown places.
My song will be the north star that leads you on the road.
It will be the pupil in your eye that lets your heart see.
And when I die and my voice is silent,
      my song will speak to you
      through how you love.

# Some Notes on These Song Offerings

#7 – I am reminded of Juan Ramon Jimenez' poem, in Robert Bly's translation:

> At first she came to me pure, dressed only in her innocence;
>     and I loved her as we love a child.
> Then she began putting on clothes she picked up somewhere;
>     and I hated her, without knowing it.
> She gradually became a queen, the jewelry was blinding. . .
> What bitterness and rage!
> . . . She started going back toward nakedness.
> And I smiled.
> Soon she was back to the single shift of her old innocence.
>     I believed in her a second time.
> Then she took off the cloth and was entirely naked . . .
> Naked poetry, always mine. I have loved that my whole life!
>                                              Juan Ramon Jimenez

I once heard Mary Oliver tell a group of aspiring poets, "Take out all the adjectives," which was her way, I think, of "refusing all ornament," the "no poetic vanity" of Tagore's poem #7. The reed flute image may have come from Rumi, the first image in his Masnavi. Surely there were Bengali translations available to him.

#12 – The ray of sunlight is a very common Sufi poetic image.

#15 – The flood image. See also the end of #57. Tagore loves the exciting, transformed, sense of landscape that comes when a river floods over its banks. He spent much of his life near rivers and on a houseboat. Here is a passage from a letter, July, 1893: "The river is rising daily. What I could see yesterday from the upper deck, I can now see from my cabin windows. Every morning I wake to find my field of vision growing larger . . . . Land and water are gradually approaching each other like two bashful lovers. The limit of their shyness has nearly been reached – their arms will soon be around each other's necks. I shall enjoy my trip along this brimful river at the height of the rains. I am fidgeting to give the order to cast off" (*Glimpses,* 59).

#20 – Tagore was very influenced by the Bauls. These wandering ecstatics of Bengal belong to a mystical tradition known as *saha-jiya (sahaj* means "simple, direct"). The Bauls' relationship to the divine mystery is personal and intimate, bypassing all doctrine, scriptures, and religions. They are not ascetics or celibates. They wander and sing songs for a living. Tagore loved their freedom from convention and their devotion to song.

#25 – He is threatened by a powerful exhaustion.

#27 – He longs for "the kind of light that comes from intense living."

#28 – He feels stunned by a stubbornness, and he prays for "release," but he is afraid that it might be given.

#29 – He has been "busy with forgetting the being I am."

#39 – He longs for a waking-up.

#40 – It will be like a compassionate rain after long drought.

#41, #47, #52, #74 – Many of these poems are written, I am told, in a woman's voice. Many others are ambiguous; a waiting is being experienced. A presence is coming near, a friend.

#52 and #53 – What is this mysterious sword-gift given by the lover?

#56, #60, and #61 – Three more things that the longed-for vision will be like:

   #58 – "Those two daft, twin brothers, life and death.
   #60 – Children playing on the beach.
   #61 – The freshness of a baby's skin.

#83, #84, #87, #88 – The most held-back, private part is a sadness. It will be the last part given in a life. The grief of separation, which is also a very creative part. The empty ruin poem, #88, also has a similar feeling.

In this mysterious sequence of poems, Tagore is determined to keep his secret. He is most clear about the absence he feels. See #88.

These poems are filled with an intense waiting. The images he finds for it in #88 are telling:

> Your presence felt in the temple ruin, . . .
> . . . a spring breeze through the toppled stone.
>     Flowers *not* brought. . . .
> . . . a worshipper looks for you,
>         longing and wandering, still refused,
>         in the empty, wall-less rooms.

And in the last lines of the sequence, the "longing and wandering" are still refused:

> You remain in the barren sanctuary, unworshipped.
>         Eternal neglect."

For the title of this book, *What Wants to Come Through Me Now*, see #89.

#90, #91, #92, #93, #94, #96, #98, #99 – A very powerful sequence of death poems. Elizabeth Kubler-Ross believed that Tagore had thought more deeply about death than anyone. Each chapter of her classic study, *On Death and Dying*, has a quotation from Tagore at its head.